MY AMAZING ADHD BRAIN

MY AMAZING ADHD BRAIN

An Hachette UK Company
www.hachette.co.uk

Vie Books, an imprint of Summersdale Publishers
Part of Octopus Publishing Group Limited
Carmelite House
50 Victoria Embankment
LONDON
EC4Y 0DZ
UK

www.summersdale.com

The authorized representative in the EEA is Hachette Ireland, 8 Castlecourt Centre, Dublin 15, D15 XTP3, Ireland (email: info@hbgi.ie)

Printed and bound in China

ISBN: 978-1-83799-126-6

This FSC® label means that materials used for the product have been responsibly sourced

Substantial discounts on bulk quantities of Summersdale books are available to corporations, professional associations and other organizations. For details contact general enquiries: telephone: +44 (0) 1243 771107 or email: enquiries@summersdale.com.

Neither the author nor the publisher can be held responsible for any loss or claim arising out of the use, or misuse, of the suggestions made herein. None of the views or suggestions in this book are intended to replace medical opinion from a doctor. If you have concerns about your health or that of a child in your care, please seek advice from a medical professional.

MY AMAZING ADHD BRAIN

A Child's Guide to Thriving with ADHD

Emily Snape

Note to parents and carers

ADHD is a very common neurodevelopmental condition that affects behaviour.

The most recognized traits people with ADHD present are inattentiveness, hyperactivity and impulsiveness.

Some children and adults may have ADD, a form of ADHD, which can cause difficulties in concentrating but not with hyperactivity. This can make it more challenging to diagnose as the behaviour is less obvious.

There is no single test to discover if someone has ADHD, but the first step if you are concerned about yourself or your child is to talk to your doctor or special educational needs lead at your child's school.

This book will help your child to:

Understand what an ADHD diagnosis can mean for them.

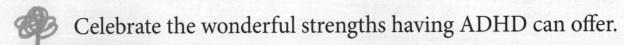 Celebrate the wonderful strengths having ADHD can offer.

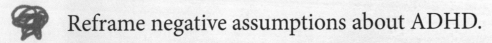 Reframe negative assumptions about ADHD.

Discover practical ideas and engaging activities.

Explore the idea of self-regulation and making mindful choices.

Hi!

I'm Pip and I have ADHD.

That stands for:

Attention Deficit Hyperactivity Disorder,

but I like to describe myself as having:

Amazing, Daring, Hard-working Determination!

Everyone with ADHD thinks and feels differently, but we can have a LOT in common.

Some of my ADHD traits make things tricky.

I find it hard to sit still in school and I can get really upset when things don't go my way. It often takes a long time to feel calm again.

But, my ADHD characteristics are the things I LOVE most about myself and actually make me EXTRA brilliant at certain things!

I would love to tell you about my special ADHD super talents and how I'm learning how to make mindful choices...

Having ADHD can help me come up with
incredible ideas!

I love model-making. My ADHD makes me really creative and I'm very good at coming up with original ideas. I want to be an inventor when I grow up!

What do you love to do?

PIP'S TIP

When I'm busy, my room can get pretty messy. It's SO annoying when I LOSE things.

I've discovered that if I take 5 minutes to tidy my room, it helps me stay organized so I can find what I'm looking for.

Having ADHD can help me have

loads of energy!

I can find it hard to sit still. Sometimes I just have to move.

I love running, jumping and skipping. You should see me in the playground!

PIP'S TIP

At school, adults can help me in lessons by:

Giving me opportunities to move around (this is often called a "movement break").

Working in a smaller room to limit distractions.

Breaking down tasks into smaller chunks.

I can also get REALLY tired in the middle of the day.

The best way to deal with this is by getting enough sleep at bedtime.

ADHD can make sleeping difficult so here's what I've learnt about how to get a grrreat night's sleep (so I can feel extra bouncy the next day)...

Ask an adult to help you make a bedtime routine that you follow every day.

Switch off screens.

Try to relax before bedtime — read a book or listen to calm music or an audiobook.

Keep regular sleep and wake times so your body clock doesn't get any surprises.

Make sure your room feels cosy. I love putting lavender under my pillow for a soothing smell.

PIP'S TIP

A weighted blanket can help you feel calm and cosy. If you don't have a weighted blanket, an adult can help by tucking a duvet in around you.

I'm having the BEST stinky sock dream!

To feel your best, you also need to make sure the food you eat is nutritious and balanced!

Delicious with water...
Eyeball ice cubes!

Super-slimy mud pie!

It is also really important to keep hydrated, so try to drink lots of water!

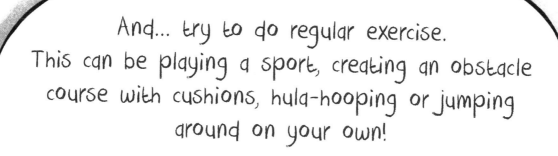

And... try to do regular exercise.
This can be playing a sport, creating an obstacle course with cushions, hula-hooping or jumping around on your own!

Exercise can help you feel more positive about facing and overcoming difficult challenges.

Having ADHD can help me

be courageous!

My ADHD sometimes makes me impulsive. I don't always think things through before I do something.

This isn't always helpful, but it does mean I'm great at taking risks. When you try new things, it develops skills and builds confidence.

I'll have a go at everything once!

PIP'S TIP

Being impulsive is brilliant, but sometimes you have to stick to routines (like getting ready for school in the morning) so you don't end up being late or feeling anxious that you haven't done something you were meant to.

Whenever you feel an urge to do something spontaneous, pause and think about whether it's the right time to act on it.

Having ADHD can help me

hyperfocus!

If I am interested in something, I can stay focused on it for AGES. My ADHD helps me feel really passionate about the things I love.

I like playing video games and the feeling I get when I master a tricky level.

I also know the name of every dinosaur discovered. My favourite dinosaur is Diplodocus!

PIP'S TIP

If I'm absorbed in something, I find it hard to stop. To help me, my dad gives me 10- and 5-minute warnings before I have to quit what I'm doing. You could also try setting an alarm to remind yourself when it is time to do something else.

PIP'S TIP

If you love video games like me, it is really important to take lots of breaks and enjoy your other passions too. Too much screen time can make you feel grouchy.

If I'm not interested in something, I can find it tricky to focus and I get distracted easily. Lots of thoughts jumble around my brain and it can be confusing and stressful.

This can be REALLY difficult when I'm in a rush or at school.

But there are all sorts of ways you can help yourself to focus...

Get organized!

So I don't forget what jobs I have to do each day, my dad sticks up reminder notes around the house.

BRUSH Teeth!

Feed fish

Make Bed

Lack of confidence

When you find things hard, it is easy to feel fed up. Don't give up. If you have a goal, take small steps to achieve it — you can do anything you put your mind to.

PIP'S TIP

A fidget toy helps me when I have to sit still. I have a box of fidget toys in my classroom for when I need them.

Having ADHD can help me

be kind!

I know first-hand how tricky things can be and how frustrating it is when they seem so easy for other monsters. This is why I am really caring and understanding – I get how hard life can feel. This makes me a super-compassionate monster.

I also love hugs!

I like hanging out with my friends but sometimes I feel like I'm the odd one out.

Here are my top friendship tips:

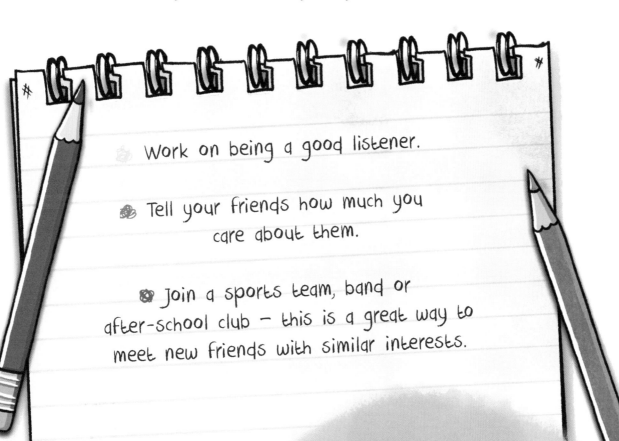

🏵 Work on being a good listener.

🏵 Tell your friends how much you care about them.

🏵 Join a sports team, band or after-school club – this is a great way to meet new friends with similar interests.

PIP'S TIP

I find it hard to take turns and that can make my friends mad. But it is SO frustrating waiting for my go. I play a lot of board games with my family which helps me develop my skills in being patient.

Low moods

When I feel down in the dumps I make myself feel better by:

- Doing star jumps
- Playing balloon volleyball
- Listening to my favourite music and dancing
- Drawing a picture
- Talking to my family
- Watching a funny video.

What makes you feel good?

PIP'S TIP

Always tell an adult you can trust when you're feeling sad or worried.

Anxiety

If you are feeling stressed, try to...

Breathe in slowly through your nose, then breathe out through your mouth and imagine you're blowing out a candle.

Count slowly in your head to 10. If you're getting distracted, you could try counting on your fingers instead.

Practise being mindful. That means focusing on what you're doing right now, rather than worrying about something in the past or what might happen in the future.

Pay attention to what you can see, smell, taste, hear and feel.

This is my worry box.
I write or draw things that make me feel anxious and post them in my box. Then I don't feel like I have to carry those worries around all the time.

Having ADHD can help me have

strong morals!

ADHD can help me recognize right from wrong. When I think something is unfair, I try to change it. I will also stand up for other monsters if I don't think they are being treated properly.

PIP'S TIP

I can get hot-headed if I don't think something is fair and this can come across as argumentative. If you feel like people aren't hearing you, count to 10 slowly. Focus on taking deep breaths and step away from the action. Once you are feeling calm, it will be a lot easier to explain your point of view.

Having ADHD can help me

be hilarious!

My busy brain comes up with lots of funny ideas. I am really proud of my zany sense of humour and I love making other monsters laugh.

Having fun helps me feel good, deal with difficult situations, make friends and help other monsters feel grrreat!

PIP'S TIP

It is important to be aware of when it is okay to be silly and when you should try to stay calm.

I am so proud of having ADHD. It is part of who I am – a fun, spontaneous, caring, passionate little monster!

I hope you can see all the ways ADHD gives me super strengths.

When I remind myself of these super strengths, I feel more confident in dealing with all the tricky challenges I face.

I hope this book has helped you too!

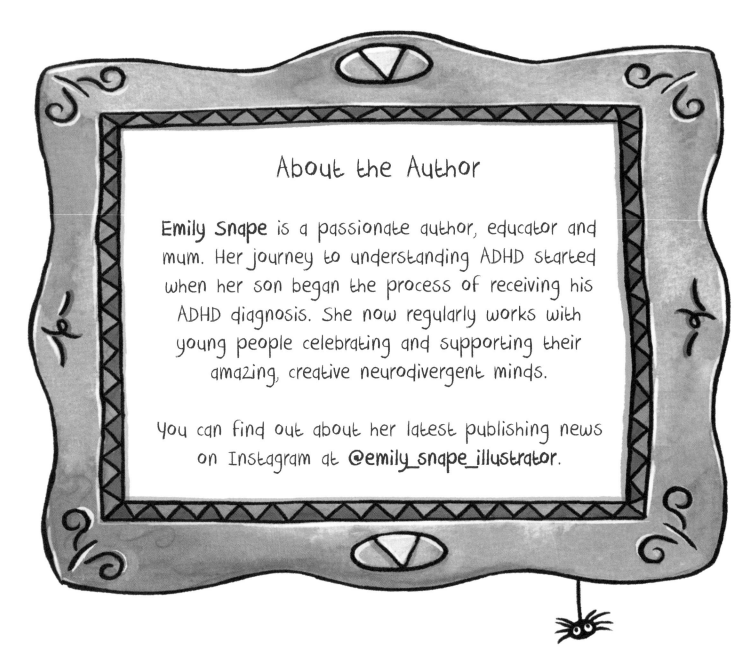

About the Author

Emily Snape is a passionate author, educator and mum. Her journey to understanding ADHD started when her son began the process of receiving his ADHD diagnosis. She now regularly works with young people celebrating and supporting their amazing, creative neurodivergent minds.

You can find out about her latest publishing news on Instagram at **@emily_snape_illustrator**.

If you're interested in finding out more about our books, find us on Facebook at **Summersdale Publishers**, on Twitter at **@Summersdale** and on Instagram and TikTok at **@summersdalebooks** and get in touch.

We'd love to hear from you!

Thanks very much for buying this Summersdale book.

www.summersdale.com